Nerdy Indigenous Art's inner Heart

Shania Richards

BookLeaf Publishing

India | USA | UK

Nerdy Indigenous Art's inner Heart ♥ ©
2022 Shania Richards

Presentation by *BookLeaf Publishing*

Web: www.bookleafpub.com

E-mail: info@bookleafpub.com

ISBN: 9789357446204

First edition 2022

DEDICATION

I dedicate this to you dear reader, for taking the time out of your busy life to truely see me like no one has before. Thank you for allowing me to be vulnerable and pour my heart out in ink. It means the world to me, just knowing no matter what you'll be able resonate with something I wrote then use that as a source to learn more. Honestly I'm grateful to share with you dear reader.

ACKNOWLEDGEMENT

Bawoo ngoonidi gamangoodoo.

With respect I would like to welcome you to the country I'm writing from, by acknowledging the deep spiritual and cultural connection of the Elders of this land: past, present and future. On which this was written.

I acknowledge Aboriginal and Torres Strait Islander People as the original inhabitants of Australia and recognise these unique cultures as part of the rich cultural heritage of all Australians.

As well as acknowledging everyone that has helped me on this adventurous Earth Journey. If it wasn't for you, I wouldn't be here today.

Yoowa walira
Bawoo.

PREFACE

The Hon, Lady Shania Janet-Shayne Richards is a 23 (years old Wongutha, Mirning, Barngarla, Ndaju, Gubrun, Bulang woman with German and British Ancestry.

Raised between Kalgoorlie, Esperance, Kambalda West, & Port Lincoln Australia. She is extremely family oriented.

Graduated from the Western Australian Academy of Performing Arts as an Aboriginal Performer, An apprentice Chef, Aspiring Author, Singer/Songwriter, Contemporary Indigenous Artist, A Cultural Heritage Consultant/Monitor (BDAC) and small business owner (Nerdy Indigenous Art).

Shania was lucky enough to have been elected the 27th Youth Governor of South Australia 2022. The first Female First Nations Regional one at that!

Reconciliation Action Plan Event

Woke up Late
Flew outta bed
I had a date
Almost hit me head
Had to wear my disguise
To meet with the big guys
Painted my face up
Like my ancestors
Ready for war
I rocked up
Walked straight thru that door
Only to find smiles behind masks
Uncle giving the acknowledgment of country
speech
My aunties paintings covered the walls
They all greeted me with hugs
As the event proceeded
I understood why I was needed
It was time to call a treaty
Sovereignty to be ceeded
Our elders need help to find peace
The youth begging for direction

Our Earth is heated
A new world order is mentioned
Australia's healing, gonna be meaty.

Paranoid Schizophrenia Diagnosis

Stuck in another hospital bed
Pop another pill
It'll help me pay the bills
Fix my head
Everyone says I'm ill
Trying to save me from a kill
Yet no one realised I was already dead.

Sexual Assault Survivor

Sitting in another waiting room

Praying that the Doctor can fix me vag

I just want to have control over my bladder
again

Trying not to cry as memories of that bad man
almost made me die

The nurse asks if I'm alright

I'll never be able to birth my own legacy

Or to pee on command

Pain free

I miss the relief

If only I never trusted that beast.

Nia from down under

Born in the desert Bushlands.
Raised throughout the ghettos.
Ocean breeze licking.
Heat kicking.
Daughter of two warring tribes.
Treaty.
Peace maker.
I was summoned by the screams of my people.
To take a stand.
Speak my truth.
Celebrate the moon.
Honour the sun.
Heal my mind, body and soul.
Become the chest piece our country is missing.
Be the one no one else wants to be.
A martyr for the cause.
A face to the movement.
Always must stay in the moment.
No longer can I hide in the shadows.
When the light wants to shine so bright from
within.
Wishin I could throw my purpose in the bin.
Nothing but a good girl.

Gods little puppet.
Surely the universe loves me.
Following the divine plan.
Completing the mission.
Honestly I'm sick of being stuck in the patterns
of karmic cycles.
Just want it all to end.
But we worked too hard.
My life has only begun.

Livin in Straya
Bronx

Neighbourhood is lit.
Bitches always getting hit.
Pain is free.
Drugs are their key.
Always see them on their knees.
Getting what they please.
Yet no one feeds the bees.
People wonder why I'm never home, always in the sea.
To cleanse my body of humanity's stupidity.
Everyone's acting brainwashed, and it hurts me.
Gonna drown my sorrows in fruity tea.
Until the Cosmos I'll soon see.

Old Soul, New Era

They call me eternal.
Recognised me as ancient.
They know all my life stories.
Yet I never met them here.
My heart bleeds knowing, they want to met.
For I am no saviour.
I am nothing special.
I am no hero.
I am no role model.
I am only doing what I've gotta do cause I want
too.
There's no gifts, no talent, no skill, no money
and no beauty.
Just struggle and hard work, from what my
anchestors gave me.
Dunno who them other mob trying to be.
Why they reaching out to me?
Singing my past names in praise.
Y'all sound so vain.
I can't save you.
You must save yourself.
I am only me.
A human being.
Like you boo.

Bad Dream

Dreamtime always telling me a story when I fall
asleep
But last night was the tale of staying with the
abuser
It was scary, because it was good.
We were happy to find each other again.
We even had a kid.
We were married and in love.
He wanted to offer me the world with a crazy
romance
Yet I am already moving on because I didn't
want to dance to the tune of DV.
The dream wouldn't release me
It took me deeper
I felt what could of been.
Something inside telling me it was all a lie.
So imagine my surprise when I woke up alive
and alone.
With nothing but tears in my eyes.

Medz

The demon in my head,
Is the one Under my bed
Where is my med

Help make it go away
Before I see my own face
Maybe this weed is just laced.

I have some memories that'll never fade
I got some regrets I'll never see
My pain is just heresy

I'm limited by my beliefs
Can't escape the illumati fate
Cause they don't exist anymore
I killed them all.

With this sweet little pill, takes away the fear.
Replenish with bliss. I urn for gods kiss.

Nurses stick another needle in my arm.
Takes my blood to feed our Queen.
Wasn't my innocence enough for the
sacramental feast.
How much of me must be spread.
Until I can finally end up dead.

Living in Australia's Bronx

Neighbourhood is lit.
Bitches always getting hit.
Pain is free.
Drugs are their key.
Always see them on their knees.
Getting what they please.
Yet no one feeds the bees.
People wonder why I'm never home, always in
the sea.
To cleanse my body of humanity's stupidity.
Everyone's acting brainwashed, and it hurts me.
Gonna drown my sorrows in fruity tea.
Until the Cosmos I'll soon see.

Old Soul. New Body.

They call me eternal.
Recognised me as ancient.
They know all my life stories.
Yet I never met them here.
My heart bleeds knowing, they want to met.
For I am no saviour.
I am nothing special.
I am no hero.
I am no role model.
I am only doing what I've gotta do cause I want
too.
There's no gifts, no talent, no skill, no money
and no beauty.
Just struggle and hard work, from what my
anchestors gave me.
Dunno who them other mob trying to be.
Why they reaching out to me?
Singing my past names in praise.
Y'all sound so vain.
I can't save you.
You must save yourself.
I am only me.
A human being.
Like you boo.

Don't compare yourself to me

Some people take drugs to get out of this world.
I take drugs to say in it.
Those people escape pain.
I make myself feel it.
Them mob cry about their trauma.
I try to heal my trauma.
Some people accept their brainwashing.
I hijacked mine, re programmed it.
Those people won't understand.
I learnt how to understand.
Them mob choose their poison.
I am trying to develop a cure.
We are not the same.
Life is a game.
Y'all can't be tamed.
Gods taking your blame.
It's a shame.
We're all so lame.
Use your bloody brains.

Letter to future self

I love you unconditionally. Thank you for everything, and for always trying your hardest and being at your best. I am very proud of the beautiful young lady you've become, and for overcoming your past challenges. Stay true to yourself, and be authentic! Continue to be unique, and have fun, exciting adventures and experiences!!! You are enough, you are worthy and you are loved.

No pride in genocide

Stop trying to make me lie
Eye eye eye
I don't give a fark
You, me, we
We we originally
Just your luck
We gonna try
Fix the colonised
We all on the same side
No one needs to die
Just trying to get by

We are the originals
And we survived

Lost

My boyfriend and I went to the electronics store to purchase a gaming PC.

A little old man came into the store, like the one from "UP". He had a walking stick and all.

 He walked around for a few minutes, rather lost. And as I watched, he built up the courage to ask the lady attendant if she can show him the iPods.

She replied that they only have the latest touch screen one, like an iPhone but for music.

He reckon nah no, I want one of those iPods for music no iPhones. She informed him that they no longer sell those ones.

And so the old man went back to being lost, in an ever changing world.

I could see how he wanted to understand this technology, but he could only ask simple humble questions.

To which received simple humble blunt answers.

About the very electronics that only existed, as this old mans life was coming to an end.

He himself was decades older than the thing he sort, which he missed by only one little decade.

My boyfriend snapped me out of this pondering by asking "Are you okay love, you look a little lost?".

Dot Painting

Today, I want to share with you something I was taught from my mother. You see, in my family we love to paint. As painting is our way of sharing our experiences, knowledge, memories and dreams. Many times for our people it was a handy tool that could save you from certain death. We've been painting for generations, and it all started as a secret coded map. We had our own secret symbols to tell other members of our culture about special places. Often our sacred sites. And within the painting we would tell a story, of how to get there and what was in that area.

We paint from the birds eye view, like stars looking down upon the Earth.

I don't like celebrities like Cardi B

I can rap and sing all her songs, but that doesn't mean I want to.

This Celebrity Has NO Shame.

Cardi B is just a glorified whore with no manners or respect for anyone else but herself.

Which is obviously why she's so full of ego and selfishness when performing.

She doesn't want to inspire others to chuck their holes around, cause she wants everyone to look at her doing it instead.

Like how rude.

You would think growing up in this male dominated society that oppressive colonial gaze would encourage her to honour womanhood, divine feminine and protect the sacred Goddess soul within.

But no, she uses it repeatedly to manipulate for money.

As seen from her previous actions as a stripper, whom Drugged and stole from many. And throughout everything she does and stands for.

Like shame job.

Her ancestors never sacrificed their lives, just for her to represent and glorify being a slut. The very thing many First Nations woman were enslaved for, and forced to be a concubine.

Now she wants to pretend that acting like one is empowering for us all?

Yeah no, maybe for an ignorant uneducated woman with no idea of the pain and trauma such an identity crisis can cause in the public eye.

What type of message is this sending to our youth?

 That what, if you wear provocative clothes, swear, strip, act anti social, and suck dick, then

you'll get the "Big" money? Like ew money
ain't shit. It's just a tool. Not worth sacrificing
your innocence for:

I just hope she realised what she's doing before
her daughter follows suit. Because my
community has no hope, all these children have
fell into that no morals, respect, manners, values,
materialistic trap. It's so bad that the little boys
(way younger than 18) are dressing up as girls to
go suck dick for crack price and her Merch. And
don't even get me started on all the underage
pregnant girls, thinking riding dick is badass.
These children should have No idea of those
adult life themes. Let children be children for
god sakes. Stop encouraging them to grow up
before their time and sexualising them.
None of these children deserve to be a dumb
whore, yet they don't want an education cause
"Cardi B didn't need it, why should we?"

God I just wish these celebrities would realise
how big their impact is upon the population and
it's impressionable youth.

The first time I saw her, the woman was on the
red carpet talking about butterflies in her vagina.
Like come on, don't be dumb. No one needed to
hear about your big hole.

If that were a man talking about his private
parts, I can bet you 💯 it would be a huge
controversy and everyone would "cancel" him.

But somehow it's okay for her to say? That's just
double standards and hypocrisy. And I'm sick of
it.

Stop making ugly hearted people famous.

It's so fake, and obvious that the mainstream
industry has its own agenda.

Psychosis

I am just going to say it like it is.

I am not a junkie, or a druggie. I'm just a gunja conasiour.

I mean sure, when I run out I get withdrawal symptoms. My skin gets all itching, and I can't help but to scratch it until blood pisses out of the genocide reminder that is my body.

Do you know what's funny?
After I was sexually abused, it was the only substance that took away the pain and severity of that trauma.

That was until the devil came out to play.

After he tormented my soul, body and mind. I found myself in a hospital bed, confided and chained up.

There was a security guard, staring at me. Like I was a ticking time bomb. He never took his poxy white colonial male gaze off of me.

I felt like a stupid crazy colonial criminal.

The Doctors forced me into the mental ward,
after they found me communicating to the
spirits.

Apparently the scientific evidence displayed that
aboriginal culture didn't count. Our beloved
beliefs and scared teachings were full of fear for
the white world.

So they silenced me with worser drugs.

Shut me up, with the fact that "my brain is
allergic to drugs."

They didn't like to debate. As I informed them
that all drugs are posion to the human body,
that's why we get the high effect. Because it's
our body fighting the toxicity of that substance.

Of course, no one likes a smart nigga.

The nurses just held me down and jabbed
needles into my arm until I stopped responding.

Of course, after a few days of this I really began
to lose touch with reality.

That Devil showed me the secrets of the universe, gave me the ability to cross the dimensions and space time to communicate with my loved ones I had lost in this third dimension.

He wasn't as bad of a bloke as the white man makes us believe.

Because once the initiation was over, I was returned back to this realm.

With the realization that There was no such thing as the white mans god, devil or money.

There is only the energy of unconditional love.

Manifesting through the buffer of our everyday lives.

And that's what truely saved me.

Not the Pot, but the potential to think for myself.

No matter how much weed I try to smoke now, it has no effect.

Only the lasting invisible universal truth.

I am, all that I am.

An energy experimenting through the essence of
love and the experience of life and beyond.

Nothing like you

What you talking bout I wanna be you?

I wanna be nothing like you.

I don't wanna walk like you.

Talk like you.

Chuck my hole around like you.

Suck dick like you.

Licking up the oppressors spit like you.

Selling out my culture like you.

Abusing privilege like you.

Bragging about money like you.

Turning the blind eye like you.

Brainwashing our kids like you.

Next time don't get it twisted, looking like a
fool.

I ain't like you boo.

No barbie wanna be here.

You so full of fear.

It's cute.

Now stay mute.

Colonial hypocrisy

"Stop blaming us for what happened to your ancestors"

BRO do you mean my GRANDMA?

Did you mean my MOTHER?!?

How far back are YOU trying to make it sound?

Enough to make you feel less guilty about the privilege of being the oppressor?

It happened in OUR LIFETIME.

Never forget it.

Because we are still haunted by the trauma.

Frank is God

Frank is always watching, always moving,
always talking and is everywhere.

Frank is everything....
Yet he is nothing,
He is infinity,
Beyond imagination
He is here, and he is there,
He is everywhere.

Behind those big gorgeous eyes is a
counciousness that is very powerful. A mask
that we frankly wear, to disguise that we are all
the same. Ancient pain. Dressed up as gain.

27th Youth Governor of South Australia, Junior Parliament Closing Ceremony Speech

I would like to thank our major sponsors for all their support for this program. And the wonderful Volunteers, Parents and Guardians who've helped make this experience possible for the participants. As they've each shown great strength, growth, passion and courage since day one of this Junior Parliment journey. I would like to remind the honourable members that they are already leaders in their own rights, and I hope they are able to take everything they've learnt here back to their schools, sporting groups and communities. On another note, I just want express my honest surprise at how engaged our South Australian Youth is about learning the nitty gritty process of creating a bill, going above and beyond to use bravery and courage to speak their truths in the chamber, as well as neautal fact sharing just to help understand another's opinion before a debate, encouraging each other to do their personal best with the utter most respect and maturity. This is the proof in the pudding, that our Youth are willing and able to make a difference where it matters the most. I honestly can't wait to see what you each accomplish and achieve from this moment forward. Leadership development doesn't stop once this session is closed. The world is now your oyster, now its time to shine & be the gorgeous pearls we witnessed you become! You all should be very proud of your growth and evolution within the program. You've come a long way, and I know you are each going to go a long way in your life journey. Just don't forget to have fun and make mistakes, because it's an important part of growth and learning. Thank you so much for participating in the 7th Session of Junior Parliment 2021. Take care, be your awesome true self and enjoy the rest of your holidays!